The Bears Wi[ll]

Jenny Nimmo
Illusrated by Lucinda Hunnam

CELEBRATION PRESS
Pearson Learning Group

Simon Smithers was fed up with home. He decided to stay outside and play with his friend Danny.

It was one of those days when the cracks in the pavement were just a bit wider than usual.

"Don't step on the cracks," said Danny, "or the bears will get you!"

"There are no bears," said Simon, which was rather a silly thing to say, because the very next moment . . .

he found himself sitting opposite three bears.

"I wish you hadn't done that," said the biggest bear.

"Done what?" said Simon in a trembling voice.

"Jumped on a crack!" said the middle-sized bear.

"I've often jumped on cracks, but this has never happened before," Simon said.

"Ah, but what did you say when you jumped on the crack?" asked the little bear.

"I . . . I said there were no bears," Simon replied, feeling rather foolish.

"You see what we mean?" The three bears wagged their claws at Simon.

By now Simon was feeling very frightened. He wished he had stayed at home.

"Nevermind," said Mrs. Bear. "You can make up for it by helping me to dust. What's your name, dear?"

"Simon," said Simon.

Just then they heard a thump on the ceiling.

"Oh, no!" moaned Mr. Bear. "Don't say it's going to happen again."

Alice Harris and her granny were coming home with the groceries. Alice was feeling angry. Granny Harris had bought lots of potatoes, and Alice kept dropping them.

"Alice, if you don't pick up those potatoes the bears will get you!" said Granny Harris.

Alice stamped her foot, right in the middle of a crack in the pavement. "There are no bears," she cried, which was rather a silly thing to say, because the very next moment . . .

she found herself sitting on top of Simon and looking at the three bears.

"You shouldn't have done that," groaned Simon.

"Done what?" asked Alice in a shaky voice.

"You stepped on a crack," Simon said.

"And you said there were no bears," added the little bear, wagging his finger at Alice.

"I'm sorry," quivered Alice, "I didn't know this would happen."

She wished she was back on Spa Drive with her grumpy granny.

"Nevermind," said Mrs. Bear. "Just get off Simon and help me with this mess. What's your name, dear?"

"Alice," said Alice.

Just then there was a tremendous bang on the ceiling. The light flickered. They all looked up.

"Oh, no!" they cried.

Ed Medwin was a moving man. He was trying to move a piano into Number 5, Spa Drive, all by himself.

"Come on, Ed," called the other men. "If you don't hurry the bears will get you!"

"There are no bears," said Ed, angrily, and he dropped one end of the piano right on a crack in the pavement, which was a rather silly thing to do, because the next moment . . .

he found himself sitting on the piano and looking at Alice and Simon and the three bears.

"What did you do that for?" growled the three bears angrily.

"What did I do?" asked Ed in a small voice.

"You dropped a piano on a crack!" said Simon.

"And you said there were no bears," said Alice, shaking her finger at him.

"So I did," said Ed. He wished he was back with his mean friends moving heavy furniture.

"Nevermind," sighed Mrs. Bear. "We won't eat you! Just help us to clear up this mess. What's your name, dear?"

"Ed," said Ed. "And I'm very sorry for all the trouble I've caused."

They moved the piano and cleaned up the living room.

Then Mrs. Bear made a nice cup of tea and generously provided her last bowl of honey.

Ed and Alice and Simon were just wondering how to eat the honey politely when . . .

a large ginger cat fell through the ceiling, right into the bowl of honey.

"We all know what you said!" cried everyone, wagging their fingers at the cat.

"Meow!" said the cat. He was very scared and very sticky, and he wished he was back on Spa Drive, being chased by a dog.

"Nevermind, Ginger," said Mrs. Bear. "We're used to a bit of fur with our honey."

And she took the cat into the kitchen and gave him a good scrub, which made him feel worse, especially as there was a great deal of thumping and banging going on above the kitchen ceiling.

"Meow," said the cat.

But Mrs. Bear didn't hear the banging because she was singing to Ginger.

Sally Simpson was a window washer. Her boss, Bill, always made her carry the bucket and the ladder.

"Come on, Sally," said Bill. "Get that ladder on to the van."

"You do it!" said Sally.

"Me? But I'm the boss," said Bill. "If you don't pick it up this minute, the bears will get you. Ha! Ha! Ha!"

"There are no bears," said Sally, and she dropped her bucket right on a crack in the pavement, which was rather a silly thing to do, because, the very next moment . . .

she found herself sitting in a kitchen sink, looking at a large bear.

"I wish you hadn't done that," said Mrs. Bear.

"Done what?" asked Sally, shivering.

Everyone else ran into the kitchen crying, "You banged your bucket on a crack and said there were no bears!"

"I'm s-s-sorry!" stuttered Sally. She wished she was back on Spa Drive with bossy Bill.

"Nevermind," said Mrs. Bear, "just take your bucket off this nice ginger cat. What's your name, dear?"

"Sally," said Sally.

She took her bucket off the cat and got out of the sink.

Then Sally, who loved cats, rubbed Ginger dry.

And the little bear, who liked being helpful, dried Sally's hair.

After this they all felt rather tired, so they decided to go to sleep in the bears' enormous bed. Then, perhaps, everything would be all right in the morning.

But, of course, it wasn't!

They hardly slept at all because there wasn't enough room and everyone woke up very early.

"What are we going to do now?" they cried.

Simon, who was a rather clever boy, said, "Why don't we all jump on the ceiling and say, 'There are bears!' Then perhaps, we'll go up instead of down!"

Everyone thought this was a very good idea.

They all stamped their feet on the ceiling and shouted, "There are bears! There are bears! THERE ARE BEARS!"

The people on Spa Drive were very frightened when they heard this. They all ran out of their houses in their nighties and pajamas and went to the police station.

Simon's idea worked, but when he and Alice and Ed and Ginger and Sally and the three bears found themselves on Spa Drive, it was quite deserted.

"I expect everyone was scared when they heard us shouting and went to the police station," said Simon.

"We'd better shout, 'There are no bears,' and then they'll come back!" Alice suggested.

"But there are bears," Mr. Bear pointed out.

"We'll go up a tree, dear," said Mrs. Bear. "Then no one will see us!"

So the three bears climbed into a tree and everyone else sat on the wall of Number 5, Spa Drive, taking care not to touch the cracks in the pavement. And they all shouted,

"There are no bears. There are no bears. THERE ARE NO BEARS!"

Then Simon's mom and dad, and Granny Harris, and the new people in Number 5, and everyone else who lived on Spa Drive, all came running back. There was a lot of hugging and kissing, and they all went indoors to have a nice cup of tea.

The three bears climbed out of the tree and stood on a crack in the pavement. Then they crossed their fingers—because bears never tell lies—and whispered, "There are no bears!"

Which was a very sensible thing to do!